W9-AGT-057

DISCARD

The History of
Video Games

Video Games and Society

The History of Video Games

Lydia Bjornlund

ReferencePoint Press®

San Diego, CA

For more information, contact:
ReferencePoint Press, Inc.
PO Box 27779
San Diego, CA 92198
www.ReferencePointPress.com

LIBRARY OF CONGRESS CATALOGING-IN-PUBLICATION DATA

Bjornlund, Lydia, 1961–
  The history of video games / by Lydia Bjornlund.
    pages cm. — (Video games and society series)
  Includes bibliographical references and index.
  ISBN-13: 978-1-60152-746-2 (hardback)
  ISBN-10: 1-60152-746-2 (hardback)
  1. Video games—History—Juvenile literature. I. Title.
  GV1469.3.B56 2015
  794.8—dc23
                                                        2014017573

Contents

The Rise of Video Games

Throughout recorded history people have created and played games. In many cultures games emerged for practical purposes, such as to develop skills and proficiencies required for more serious endeavors such as hunting or warfare. As human society became more urban, games evolved to fill the time and make social connections.

As digital technology moved beyond industry and science, people have integrated it into their leisure activities and game playing. The large mainframe computer gave rise to the earliest video games—simplistic games that computer scientists used to test their programming ability rather than to provide people with entertainment. As computer programmers became more familiar with computers, however, they began to recognize their possibilities as entertainment vehicles. Thus, each advance in computers has led to new approaches to game development and new types of games. The personal computer has brought video games into people's homes; the Internet, mobile phones, and tablets then made gaming portable. Video games have spread across multiple platforms to reach a greater number of players.

Today's video games have infiltrated every aspect of popular culture. The Entertainment Software Association (ESA) states that 58 percent of Americans play video games, and 51 percent of US households own at least one dedicated game console (households that own game consoles own an average of two.) Video games have changed how humans play games and introduced new types of competition.

The development of video games has not followed a simple or linear route. Video game development required the creation of new platforms and technologies as well as the games themselves. Therefore, video game design has impacted the evolution of computing, the visual creativity of game artists, the manner in which people understand and relate to three-dimensional virtual worlds, and a host of other technological and imaginative aspects of modern life. "Defining the limits of what is meant by 'video game' is more complicated than it first appears," notes Mark J.P. Wolf, a professor in the Communication Department at Concordia University–Wisconsin. "Differing aspects, such as technology, art, and the nature of the experience need . . . [to] be considered in defining the term."[1] Indeed, video games might seem like simple amusements, but their success depends on the seamless integration of a number of unique aspects: technology, art, video, sound, and, of course, the fun of the game itself.

Video games have distinctly different characteristics in large part because there have been many paths to their development. Computer scientists, game developers, hardware engineers, software engineers, graphic artists, and many others have played important roles in the history of video games, finding uniquely different ways to address processing speed, graphical display, memory, and other technological limitations.

The market, too, has played an important role in the development of video games. The multicolored, pixelated blobs marching around the screens of early games looked that way not because of lack of imagination but because of the limitations of technology; technology that would have allowed more intriguing video or graphics came only at an astronomical cost. This is perhaps one of the most important factors in the development of video games: market economics. Each successful innovation in the field was prompted by commercial viability. The most successful games and consoles have never been those with the most advanced technology. Rather, they have been affordable options offering the best variety and perceived value. Early on, these were mostly arcade games that could leverage the expense of their development by spreading the cost among large numbers of users. Later technologies made personal computers and home consoles affordable to the average family, bringing video games into the home.

A Global Controversy

The result is a vast array of video games that delight, obsess, and frustrate people of all ages, genders, and segments of society. For many

Early video games were constrained more by technology's limits than imagination. It was too cost-prohibitive to design games with exciting and detailed features. Pictured is Atari's Pong, *which was simple but fun and available to the masses at a reasonable cost.*

they are sheer joy. But for others they have become a hazard, blamed for problems ranging from obesity to a decline in morality. Some critics view many video games as violence simulators, prompting players to act out aggression in the real world. The common complaint is that many players—especially young players—cannot separate video game worlds from the world around them and therefore carry over violent fantasies into daily experience. Other critics maintain that spending too much time in virtual worlds keeps players from coping with real-world problems and developing social skills necessary to manage interpersonal relationships. Nick Yee, a research scientist who studies gamer behavior writes:

> When video games get into the news, they are almost always framed using two deeply entrenched yet diametrically opposed [positions]. When we insist that games turn innocent boys into criminals, gaming is perceived as a deviant teenage activity. But 58% of Americans play video games, their average age is 30, and it is a social activity for 62% of these gamers. And when we insist that virtual worlds are detached from reality, we ignore all the unexpected and fascinating ways in which virtual worlds change us and what it means to be human in a digital world.[2]

Although the fears of video game addiction are real, a number of research studies have shown that playing video games may accrue considerable benefits in terms of high-level strategic thinking, spatial awareness, eye-hand coordination, and more. To some observers, these important skills are often translated from video worlds to the real world, improving brain function and logical reasoning.

Whatever controversies surround video games, it is clear that they are here to stay. The appeal of video games has expanded far beyond the stereotype to attract users of both genders and all ages, ethnicities, and socioeconomic demographics. According to the Entertainment Software Association, the decade has witnessed a continual increase in the number of female gamers. In 2013, over 45 percent of game players were women or girls. Casual and social network gaming have been primary factors in the increase of female gamers, but it has also been the result of an interest on the part of video game developers to attract a wider audience. "Indeed when you take into account mobile games like *Angry Birds* and *Plants vs. Zombies*,

"58% of Americans play video games, their average age is 30, and it is a social activity for 62% of these gamers."[2]

—Nick Yee, research scientist at Ubisoft.

and social games like *FarmVille* and *Words With Friends*, suddenly you realize that even your mother-in-law who churns her own ice cream and your technologically challenged uncle are hardcore gamers,"[3] writes Greg Perrault, a media researcher at the University of Missouri.

Video games have advanced beyond what early developers could have imagined. And as advances in technology become more affordable, there will no doubt be exciting new developments in the video game industry. Perhaps in the near future gamers may truly be able to lose themselves in a virtual world, leaving behind the stresses of everyday life to live vicariously through virtual selves. Video games may advance to the point that will allow living, feeling avatars who can experience a virtual world in all its artificial splendor. Only time will tell.

From the Laboratory to Main Street

Chapter One

In the mid-1950s the idea of spending hours in front of a computer screen playing a game was unimaginable. Computers were giant machines operated by entire teams of scientists dedicated to serious, scientific research. Using such complex and expensive technology for something as frivolous as playing a game would have seemed ludicrous. Few could have predicted the rapid advances in technology that would bring the computer into the home as a platform for millions to play video games.

Within just a couple of decades computers had become smaller and easier to use than their room-sized ancestors. Like the television before it, the personal computer moved from being a novelty that only the rich could afford to a seeming necessity. At the same time, video games entered the market. Through the unique combination of luck, experimentation, timing, and vision, video games soon found their way into everyday life as well.

Early Experiments

The earliest video games developed as an accidental offshoot of computer research into artificial intelligence, adaptive learning, and military strategy. Computers developed as "counting machines"—or sophisticated calculators. As computer technology advanced during the Second World War, code-breakers used these machines to help translate encoded enemy communications. The manipulations of these codes would form the basis for what became computer code. Soon several computer languages emerged from this code, which served as the building blocks for all subsequent computer programs—or software—including video games.

In 1949 the Electronic Delay Storage Automatic Calculator (ED-SAC) computer became the first computer to run a program from memory. Stored-program computers were successfully commercialized in 1951 by computer pioneers J. Presper Eckert and John Mauchly, making it possible for academic institutions, research organizations, and corporations to adopt mainframes. Soon there were multiple contenders vying for a share of this burgeoning market. Sometimes referred to as "IBM and the Seven Dwarfs," the main computer designers of the time were Burroughs, UNIVAC, NCR, Control Data, Honeywell, General Electric, RCA, and, of course, IBM. There were several obstacles to the adoption of computers and related technology, however. They were extremely expensive. In today's dollars, a computer with the same power as today's laptop might cost half a million dollars; the more expensive ones typically used by researchers ran into the millions. These computers were huge. They required a large room that had to be cooled to keep the computers from overheating. Even the best computers burned out frequently, and moths were attracted to the machines, causing them to short-circuit. (Today's computer programmers still speak of "debugging" their computer programs.) The computers needed a team of skilled operators and experts who could fix the computers when they crashed. Such complex, expensive machines were not for games but for serious scientific research.

Thus, early video game programming developed as a means of testing scientific theories. The earliest computer scientists used logic puzzles, board games, card games, and military simulations to test computer capability. These games advanced the understanding of how computers and other technology could be used to create video games, but the limitations of computers prohibited commercial use.

Two of the first games to be circulated beyond their developers were *Nim*, a mathematical game played on a computer built specifically for display at the 1951 Festival of Britain, and *OXO*, a tic-tac-toe game that University of Cambridge PhD student Alexander S. Douglas programmed in 1952 as part of his thesis. *OXO* was the earliest known game to display graphics on a monitor. Meanwhile, other developers sought to replicate board games. In 1956 Arthur Samuel at IBM created a computerized checkers game, which became a sensation after it was shown on television. Americans were intrigued not only by the novelty of a computer game but also by the fact that the computer was capable of defeating even the most skilled check-

In the 1950s stored-program computers were successfully commercialized making large mainframes available to academic institutions and corporations. The UNIVAC (pictured) was the first computer designed for commercial use and led to the creation of video games.

ers players. Two years later Carnegie Mellon University researchers developed the Newel-Shaw-Simon (NSS) Chess Program, the first chess program to defeat a human opponent. (In fairness, the program defeated a player who had been taught the rules of the game just two hours before the match.)

Tennis, Anyone?

But it was *Tennis for Two* that set the proverbial ball in motion. Created by physicist William Higinbotham and his lab technician Robert Dvorak to entertain guests at the Brookhaven National Laboratory's annual visitors' day in 1958, *Tennis for Two* displayed a tennis court in side view. Two players played the game using box-shaped controllers equipped with a knob for trajectory and a button for hitting the

Pong and Its Legacy

Pong was among the earliest video game hits. Simple by today's standards, the game allowed two players to rotate knobs to control the vertical movement of on-screen paddles to hit a digital "ball" back and forth. *Pong* was first released in 1972 as an arcade came, but its staggering success led Atari to sign a deal with Sears to introduce a home console version. Like the arcade version, the Tele-Games *Pong* home console caught on instantly. It was Sears' top-selling item for Christmas 1974.

Pong's success assured its place in history but also widespread imitation: General Instruments created a circuit that held an exact clone of *Pong* along with several variations of the game for use on home televisions. Other companies soon were buying this chip and rebranding *Pong* for their own arcade booths. At the height of its popularity, *Pong* was played on at least five hundred differently named systems released by more than three hundred different producers, earning it a coveted spot in the history of video games.

"ball." *Tennis for Two* pointed to the future of video game development in terms of subject matter, ease of use, and the adaptation of new technology.

Despite its revolutionary approach, the development of *Tennis for Two* was haphazard at best. Higinbotham and Dvorak hooked up relays and transistors to a $200,000 computer and oscilloscope usually used for complex mathematical calculations. An oscilloscope plots voltages of a given electronic signal or signals as a dot (or a series of dots—a wave) on a two-dimensional display. Interviewed at the fiftieth anniversary of the game's first airing, Higinbotham's son reminisced about the development of *Tennis for Two:* "My dad liked the game . . . but in a way he cheated. He saw in the oscilloscope instructions that you could manipulate the dot on the screen. In his mind, it became a tennis ball. It took just a few hours to go from [this] to an interactive game."[4] To be precise, it took three weeks to build and two days to work out the bugs.

While extremely popular with the public, the game was ultimately dismantled and its parts repurposed. Like most game creators in the 1950s, Higinbotham never considered commercialization. His goal was research, not entertainment. As the widespread adoption of computers moved from serious academics to their students, however, games became an end in themselves.

Computers Go to College

Some of the early advances in computer science took place at the Massachusetts Institute of Technology (MIT), which by 1960 was one of the world's leading centers for computer research. The Lincoln Laboratory at MIT had a custom-built experimental computer called the TX-0. Smaller and more interactive than MIT's more powerful mainframes, the TX-0 also had fewer restrictions. While small by today's standards, at the time the TX-0 was extremely impressive.

It had a graphical (twelve-inch oscilloscope) display screen—one of the first computers with a graphical user interface—and a data reader that "read" punched tape for instructions. The TX-0 also had a 16-bit central processing unit (CPU)—the "brains" of the computer—much more flexible and nimbler than the MIT's huge IBM mainframes. Bit is short for "binary digit," a basic unit of information that can only have two values, such as "0 or 1" or "on or off." In processing terms, this refers to the number of distinct patterns a unit can store: a 1-bit processor can store two patterns (0 or 1), a 2-bit processor can store four (00, 01, 10, or 11), and so forth. The number of possible patterns doubles for each bit, so a 16-bit processor can store up to 65,536 distinct patterns. Computer processors decode strings of bits to perform tasks. The term is also used to represent graphic capabilities of computers by indicating how many bits are within a given dot on the screen. For example, an 8-bit image can generate 256 distinct colors; a 24-bit image can display over 16 million colors—enough to simulate what the human eye can detect. The dot on the screen is a pixel, a shorthand term for picture element—the smallest sample of an image.

> "My dad . . . saw in the oscilloscope instructions that you could manipulate the dot on the screen. In his mind, it became a tennis ball. It took just a few hours to go from [this] to an interactive game."[4]
>
> —William Higinbotham Jr., son of Tennis for Two creator William Higinbotham.

Until the arrival of the TX-0, computers everywhere had been reserved almost exclusively for "serious" scientists, researchers, mathematicians, and academics, but MIT students were allowed to use the TX-0 during off-peak hours at night. This rare privilege soon attracted a group of engineering undergraduate students who referred to themselves as "hackers." (They used the word *hack* as slang to describe a particularly clever feat of ingenuity.) Soon, hackers were spending their nights punching out computer code on paper tape to create improved programming tools, music programs, and simple games like *Mouse in a Maze* and *Tic-Tac-Toe*.

In 1961 the aging TX-0 at MIT was joined by a PDP-1, a computer that was equipped with a high-quality vector display, providing better graphical capabilities and sharper, less blurry images. Inspired by the science-fiction novels of E.E. Smith, Steve Russell, a computer science student at MIT, created a game in which two human-controlled spaceships attempt to destroy each other. Russell programmed *Spacewar!* not to sell to a waiting market but rather to demonstrate his computer wizardry and prowess to his peers, but computer manufacturer DEP decided to include it as a test program on PDP-1. Writer Stewart Brand remarks in *Rolling Stone* magazine ten years later: "Spacewar . . . was the illegitimate child of the marrying of computers and graphic displays. It was part of no one's grand scheme. It served no grand theory. It was the enthusiasm of irresponsible youngsters. It was disreputably competitive. . . . It was merely delightful. Spacewar . . . was a flawless crystal ball of things to come in computer science and computer use."[5]

"Spacewar . . . was a flawless crystal ball of things to come in computer science and computer use."[5]

—*Stewart Brand, author and editor of the* Whole Earth Catalog.

By 1969 *Spacewar!* could be found in university computer labs across the United States. But *Spacewar!* did far more than provide entertainment: it inspired the nation's budding computer experts to experiment. *Spacewar!* soon had spawned hundreds of variants as well as entirely new games. Despite the popularity of these games, they remained in the lab. Some adherents of *Spacewar!* appreciated its potential, but the hardware was simply too expensive to make it commercially viable: a basic PDP-1 cost $120,000 (over

$720,000 in today's dollars). As computers and components became more affordable, the dream of commercial video games became more realistic.

Ralph Baer: The Father of Video Games

A creative genius named Ralph Baer was among the first who sought a route to commercial viability for video games. As early as 1951, with television still in its infancy, Baer recognized the potential for using television as an interactive medium for playing games. It took years to bring the potential to reality, but in 1966 Baer created the Brown Box, the first home video game console. As an engineer for Sanders Associates, a defense contractor in Nashua, New Hampshire, Baer moved that company into the world of electronics.

While Sanders Associates funded Baer's initial project, finding a viable manufacturing partner proved challenging. After initial agreements with a cable company fell through in 1968, Baer approached

Engineer Ralph Baer is seen playing with the Brown Box he created in 1966. This was the first home video game console. Baer eventually made an agreement with Magnavox to bring it to market, setting the foundation for the modern home video game industry.

every television manufacturer in America. Many were skeptical; others were too greedy for Baer to accept their terms. Eventually Magnavox and Baer came to an agreement, and in 1972 they launched the Magnavox Odyssey, the first video game device made for consumers. The Magnavox retailed at one hundred dollars and for many years was Sanders' most lucrative product. Baer followed up with additional games, expanding into new types of accessories and peripherals, such as a light gun. Baer's ideas would set the foundation for other developers, giving rise to everything from cable television game downloads to wireless controllers and forever earning him the moniker of "father of video games."

Arcade Games

In comparison to the PDP-1's *Spacewar!* the Magnavox Odyssey was rudimentary. But it succeeded where *Spacewar!* could not because a system that could support a program with the sophistication of *Spacewar!* was much too expensive for consumers. On their way to America's homes, sophisticated computer games would first make a stop in strip malls, bars, and restaurants, where new coin-operated video games became the mainstay of the video arcade.

> "You can't say that video games grew out of pinball, but you can assume that video games wouldn't have happened without it. It's like bicycles and automobiles."[6]
>
> —Steven Baxter, former producer of CNN Computer Connection.

The coin-operated amusement industry was already well established by the time video games arrived. Coin-operated mechanical amusements and skill games such as pinball were popular in gaming parlors, in bars, and at fairgrounds. "You can't say that video games grew out of pinball, but you can assume that video games wouldn't have happened without it," notes Steven Baxter, the former producer of *CNN Computer Connection*. "It's like bicycles and automobiles."[6] By the 1960s a renaissance in use of technology that could fire light rays (missiles) across a screen gave rise to driving and target-shooting games. Sega's *Periscope* and Chicago Coin's *Speedway* were among the games that pioneered the adoption and integration of elaborate electromechanical devices, visual displays, electronic sound effects, and music into an interactive and fun experience for gamers.

Mario: The Birth of a Legend

Mario—a short, pudgy, Italian plumber with blue overalls and a red cap and shirt—is today as recognizable as Mickey Mouse and has become the mascot not only of Nintendo but of the whole video game industry. Since the introduction of Mario in *Donkey Kong* in 1981, the Mario franchise has sold more than 210 million units, making it the best-selling video game franchise of all time.

Legendary video game creator Shigeru Miyamoto invented Mario while developing *Donkey Kong*. Nintendo had sought to secure the license for a Popeye game with the characters Popeye, Bluto, and Olive Oyl. When this was unsuccessful, Miyamoto sought to create a similar love triangle with Mario, Donkey Kong, and Pauline. In the early stages of *Donkey Kong*'s development, Mario's focus had merely been to escape a maze. However, Miyamoto enabled Mario to jump and added rolling barrels to the game.

Due to the graphical limitations of hardware at the time, Mario's clothes were designed to contrast with the background. A red cap was added to avoid having to draw the intricacies of hairstyle, forehead, and eyebrows, as well as to avoid having to animate Mario's hair as he jumped. Mario's appearance has become more refined over time, and the original colors of his shirt and overalls have been reversed, but he continues running, jumping, and dodging his way into the hearts of gamers worldwide.

Nolan Bushnell, an engineering student at the University of Utah, was among the visionaries who advanced video games beyond these rudimentary games. He happened to have been exposed to *Spacewar!* at the university at the same time that he was working at the coin-operated games section of the Lagoon Amusement Park. Entrepreneurial by nature, Bushnell enlisted Ted Dabney, an older and more experienced engineer, to help him develop a new game based on the principles of *Spacewar!* Using a minicomputer proved prohibitively expensive, so Bushnell was forced to consider a new path: controlling a television's cathode-ray tube to move dots around a screen. The game had two rotational knobs for direction, a "thrust" button for acceleration, and a "fire" button to release missiles. To develop and market their idea, Bushnell and Dabney formed Syzygy Engineering. The resulting *Computer Space* effectively translated the concepts behind *Spacewar!* into a coin-operated arcade game housed within a stand-up cabinet. The game was hardwired into the components of the unit itself, which used a fifteen-inch, black-and-white portable television with specifically modified diode arrays.

Computer Space seemed to have all the elements needed for success, but its controls proved to be overly complicated for the average consumer. "I loved it, and all my friends loved it, but all my friends were engineers," says Bushnell. "It was a little too complicated for the guy with the beer in the bar."[7] In short, *Computer Space* was a commercial failure: Syzygy failed to sell even the entire production run. But Bushnell had learned an invaluable lesson in the process: video games needed to be easy to play. At the same time, however, they had to be challenging to encourage repeat play. Henry Jenkins, the director of the Comparative Media Studies Program at MIT, puts it this way: "The worst thing a kid can say about homework is that it is too hard. The worst thing a kid can say about a game is it's too easy."[8]

> "The worst thing a kid can say about homework is that it is too hard. The worst thing a kid can say about a game is it's too easy."[8]
>
> —Henry Jenkins, director of Comparative Media Studies at MIT.

Pong Goes to the Arcade

Undaunted by these initial obstacles, in 1972 Bushnell and Dabney founded Atari, Inc. Their goal was to find a commercially viable video game. *Pong* would prove to be everything they were looking for, and more.

Developed by Atari engineer Allan Alcorn as a training exercise, the prototype for *Pong* was basic: a four-foot wooden cabinet with a black-and-white television and hand-soldered circuit boards to control the game. Built on the basic ping-pong game, *Pong* players turned a dial to move a virtual paddle and deflect an oncoming ball toward the opponent's side of the screen. Alcorn's *Pong* also added digital sound effects, divided the paddle into eight segments to change the ball's angle of return, and increased the ball's speed the longer it remained in play. *Pong* could be played against another live player or a computer opponent. Easy to play, it quickly achieved unprecedented success: more than nineteen thousand arcade machines were sold over the next decade.

Pong's success spawned many direct imitations and inspired developers to create new games using the same basic game-play concepts. The next decade saw the propulsion of video game cabinets into the mainstream. From their roots in Silicon Valley, arcade video games spread across the Pacific to Japan, spurring international competition and a video game race that led to increasingly sophisticated graphics, sound, and game play.

One of the first games to break the mold was *Gun Fight* (known as *Western Gun* in Japan and Europe), an arcade shooter game released in 1975 by the Japanese game company Taito. The game introduced discrete game characters and a theme: users controlled two Old West cowboys armed with revolvers facing off in a duel. Subsequent designers improved upon the game by using a microprocessing chip that vastly improved graphics and enabled smoother animation.

Invading Home Space

Another Nishikado and Taito game, *Space Invaders*, revolutionized the fledgling arcade video game. Like *Gun Fight*, *Space Invaders* utilized an Intel processor, but it added pixel-based graphics on a television monitor, sound-generated custom circuitry, and an advanced sound chip. Nishikado not only designed and programmed the game but also created the artwork, engineered the arcade hardware, and assembled the microcomputer from scratch.

Space Invaders introduced the world to hordes of pixelated aliens that the player must destroy with a mobile laser cannon. Success brought on new challenges, as the aliens (moving according to the beat of the sound track) marched ever faster down the screen. In earlier games, music had generally been limited to introductory and "game over" sequences; *Space Invaders* used a four-note theme throughout the entire game, superimposed with the sound effects of missile fire and exploding aliens.

The innovative approach brought unparalleled success, as *Space Invaders* attracted young people to bars and mall arcades nationwide

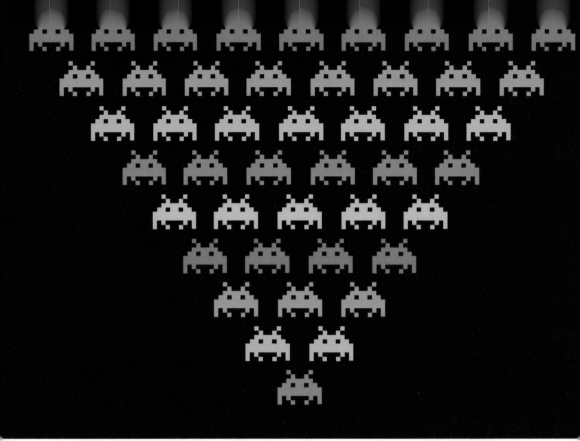

Games like Space Invaders, *with its lines of pixelated aliens marching down the screen, revolutionized the fledgling arcade video market. The game's addictive simplicity attracted people—who otherwise would have ignored such childish amusements—to bars and malls nationwide.*

to compete for the highest score. Recognizing the potential of the game, Atari bought the rights to convert it for the Atari 2600, quadrupling the sales of the console. The pixelated enemy alien soon became a pop culture icon, and the game's addictive simplicity attracted many people who otherwise might have ignored such childish amusements. "I came home from college to find my mother addicted to the game," says Linda Barton, who went to college in the early 1980s. "She spent hours wiping out row after row of aliens. When I tried to beat her top score, I could see how much time she'd been playing."[9]

The success of such simple, addictive games spurred dozens of developers to create and manufacture new video games. The burgeoning of affordable home computers in the late 1970s and early 1980s contributed to the trend, as personal computers allowed individual programmers and hobbyists to develop games in their spare time. Owing to their graphical simplicity and the memory limitations of the machines on which games were played, early games were easy to produce. Often, they were developed by one person, who designed the game play, created the graphics, and programmed the sound effects. Many early programmers merely copied the idea of *Space Invaders* to create other shooting games, but others experimented with new concepts and technologies. The result was the proliferation of games in a wide variety of genres, from puzzle and strategy games to more unique platform games. In 1981, for example, Nintendo, a Japanese company formed almost a century earlier as a card company, released *Donkey Kong*, a new type of game in which skill and timing were more important than speed. With these games, Nintendo introduced iconic characters that remain part of the culture of video games to this day.

Entrepreneurs sought to capitalize on the popularity of arcade games to capture the family market as well. In fact, it was video game guru Nolan Bushnell who in 1977 founded the predecessor to the highly successful Chuck E. Cheese's franchise. Chuck E. Cheese's Pizza Time Theatre was labeled as the first family restaurant to integrate food with an indoor arcade. By March 2014 Chuck E. Cheese's had grown into a multimillion-dollar company; its 577 franchises continue to provide video game entertainment for children.

The arcade game industry reached its peak in 1982. In that year it generated $8 billion—more than the revenue of the music ($4 billion) and film ($3 billion) industries combined. But just when the arcade industry seemed invincible, there arose a new competitor: portable consoles and gaming computers that did not require the cabinet space of the arcade models. Video games were coming home.

Video Gaming
Comes Home

Chapter Two

If the early history of video games was driven by big personalities and big ideas, the development of consoles was about companies making small ideas work. As Baer's early experience with his Brown Box illustrates, creating a console was the easy part. Translating the console into a product that suited the whims of the consumer market would prove infinitely more challenging.

The First Home Console

The history of the home console began in 1972, when Ralph Baer and Magnavox introduced the Odyssey, a video game console that included several built-in games and could be connected to any television set. The console had no central processing unit (CPU) to interpret and manage game codes. The games for the system were imprinted on cards that simply allowed certain connecting pins to establish signals that registered as commands to designate the dynamics of play. Each game came with a plastic overlay that attached directly to the TV screen and showed the environment the pixels could traverse. Erkki Huhtamo, a media historian and professor at the University of California, suggests that Magnavox executives did not recognize the game-changing nature of Baer's box: "The Magnavox Odyssey . . . was more than just a clever product, although its producers may not have fully noticed the momentous nature of the transformation they helped to initiate. To Magnavox, the little device may have been just an accessory to the television set, a way to give the TV new uses and solidify their own business opportunities."[10]

Driven by the extraordinary popularity of Atari's *Pong*, in 1975 Magnavox released a scaled-down version (the Odyssey 100) that played just *Pong* and hockey, and a slightly more sophisticated console (the Odyssey 200) that added onscreen scoring to these games as well as a third game (*Smash*) and allowed up to four players to join in the fun.

Released almost simultaneously, *Pong* and the two Magnavox Odyssey consoles ignited the consumer video game market and spurred dozens of other entrepreneurial companies to get in on the action. Many of the new players had no background in television manufacturing or consumer electronics. Coleco, for instance, started as a shoe-leather company, flirted with above-ground swimming pools in the 1950s, and had become a leading snowmobile manufacturer when it introduced the Telstar video game console in 1976.

These early console systems had inherent limitations, most of which were related to the challenges of creating systems that could play multiple games without using a CPU. Each of the main manufacturers compensated in a different way. Atari's games were hardwired into the console unit, Magnavox cartridges activated different game circuits within the console, and the Telstar was an empty shell that required all the game components to be incorporated into the game cartridges. It was Robert Noyce, who would later found the computer chip manufacturing giant Intel, who hit on a better solution with the Fairchild Channel F. Unlike earlier systems, the Fairchild Channel F had a programmable microprocessor, which meant that its cartridges needed just a single read-only memory (ROM) chip to store game instructions. Read-only memory is a form of digital information storage that can be read but not altered, which makes it ideal for games that follow rules. For the first time, game instructions could be hardwired into the cartridges and accessed when connected to the CPU, which processed the codes and actually ran the game. The cartridge containing the codes could be separate from the console, and the interchangeable game was born.

Innovation inspired imitation. Within a year Atari and leading television manufacturer RCA had released cartridge-based consoles, but the market was initially unreceptive. In its first year the Atari VCS (later renamed the Atari 2600) sold fewer units than its production run. Meanwhile, to clear stock, manufacturers of obsolete consoles sold their systems at a loss. This sudden flooding of the market during a period of recession forced smaller game companies out of business. RCA and Fairchild both abandoned their game consoles, leaving Atari and Magnavox as the only contenders in the home console market.

If these companies were gambling on the market to catch on to home gaming, their gamble paid off. In 1980 Atari released its console version of the arcade hit *Space Invaders* for the Atari 2600. Like the arcade version, the home version of *Space Invaders* met with unprecedented commercial success, pushing console sales above 2 million units and providing Atari with over $2 billion in profits that year. The success of Atari's gamble initiated two trends: console manufacturers began to seek exclusive rights to arcade titles, and console manufacturers advertised to consumers that they could bring the arcade experience home.

Atari Struggles and Flops

In 1976 Nolan Bushnell sold Atari to Warner Communications. The move proved devastating for Atari. Born of innovation, the company shifted its emphasis to profit—a quest that undermined the quality and integrity of its products. Warner refused to give credit to developers of its best-selling games for fear that competitors would steal its talent. Internal memos circulated after Bushnell's departure showed that the games developed by four people—David Crane, Bob Whitehead, Alan Miller, and Larry Kaplan—had accounted for more than half the company's game revenues. In a 2010 *IGN Magazine* interview, Crane recalls: "So we four guys making about $30,000 a year made Atari $60 million? There's something wrong here!"[11] The so-called "Gang of Four" left Atari in 1979 to found Activision, a game company that charged premium prices for new game cartridges for the Atari 2600. Gutted of its prime developers, Warner's Atari division suffered creatively and, consequently, financially.

Warner Communications bet on the concept of linking computer games to popular culture. In 1982 it introduced an *E.T.* game based on the blockbuster movie. Securing the rights to the *E.T.* title had been a drawn-out and expensive undertaking that left less than six weeks for Atari developers to create the game in time for the 1982 Christmas season. The result was a game that was substandard by almost every measure—including commercial success. Atari sent 5 million cartridges to distributors and "nearly all of them came back"[12] la-

In 1982 Atari and Warner Communications introduced an E.T. game based on the blockbuster movie. The game was rushed through development to make the Christmas season. The substandard game was a commercial flop.

mented Atari's president. Just five hundred thousand copies sold that Christmas and another 1 million in total. Copies could not even be sold at a loss, and truckloads of unopened cartridges ended up buried beneath a layer of concrete in a New Mexico landfill. Atari chalked up a loss of $310.5 million in the second quarter of 1983, largely because of the *E.T.* debacle.

The disaster shook up the video game industry. Both consumers and retailers moved away from consoles, leaving manufacturers with thousands of unsold units. Many would-be game developers found more stable jobs; those who remained often worked only part-time. Creating games became more of a hobby than a profession. Several

Nintendo: How One Company Changed an Industry

Perhaps the most important lessons to be learned from Nintendo are adaptation and persistence. Nintendo, which is today perhaps the most prolific and successful video game manufacturer in the world, began over a century ago as a playing card company. In the face of declining card sales, in 1956 the founder's grandson traveled to the United States to acquire licenses to put Disney characters on Nintendo playing cards to boost business. By 1963 the enterprise was dwindling, so Nintendo refocused on the Japanese toy industry and transferred to the video games market in 1974.

While not an instant success, Nintendo tried its hand at arcade and console games before its first hits: *Game & Watch* (a hand-held video game series) in 1980 and the 1981 arcade hit *Donkey Kong*. Nintendo took weaknesses and transformed them into strengths. The NES's limited memory, for example, meant that creating a whole new character icon was not possible when expanding popular games such as *Donkey Kong*, so Nintendo's developers simply changed the colors of Mario's shirt from red to green, creating his twin brother Luigi for *Mario Bros.* in 1983.

Nintendo kept its internal development teams independent, self-sufficient, and compact, focusing on good ideas, appealing characters, and the pursuit of fun. While many competitors sought higher complexity, Nintendo erred on the side of simplicity, constantly bucking trends to keep their prices competitive. The GameBoy, for example, won the market war over much more sophisticated hand-helds because the games were good and the unit was comparatively inexpensive.

US video game companies filed for bankruptcy in 1983. Most of the companies that survived moved on to other industries. When veteran video game programmer and entrepreneur Jon Freeman was asked in a 1984 interview whether game design was a means to achieve fame and fortune, he replied: "Not unless your idea of fame is having your name recognized by one or two astute individuals. I've been making a living (after a fashion) designing games [but] I wouldn't recommend it for someone with a weak heart or a large appetite."[13]

Japan Takes on the World Market

As American video game companies were going under, Nintendo was emerging as a viable contender. In 1983 Nintendo released in Japan the Famicom, which would be renamed the Nintendo Entertainment System, or NES, in the United States. Supporting high-resolution images, larger color palettes, and tiled backgrounds that provided for more detail and variety, NES games were longer and more visually appealing than their predecessors. Because US consumers had written off video games as a passing fad, Nintendo advertised the NES not as a video game but as a toy. This did not stop their appeal for adults, however. "My wife bought this for me on my 30th birthday," reminisces one user on the thirtieth anniversary of the NES's release. "It was the best birthday present ever. Many nights we would stay up until 3 [o'clock] playing Super Mario 3 before getting up at 7 to go to work. You would not believe how many quarters I had put into video games for 15 years previous to that."[14]

Featuring a front-loading cartridge port similar to a video tape recorder and including a plastic "robot," the NES quickly became the highest-selling console in America and almost singlehandedly revitalized the video game market. "By Christmas 1986, the Nintendo Entertainment System was the hottest toy on the market," write Carl Shapiro and Hal R. Varian in a *Harvard Business Press* article. "The very popularity of the NES fueled more demand and enticed more game developers to write games . . . making the system yet more attractive."[15]

Nintendo's secret was twofold. First, Nintendo required developers to sign a contract agreeing not to develop games for anyone else. By legally binding developers to the NES, Nintendo ensured exclusivity and quality control of the end product, consolidating their brand in the minds of users and making Nintendo synonymous with its games. The second element of Nintendo's success was the novelty of the games themselves. Nintendo's unique characters, such as Mario, became icons that carried over from game to game across various series. In Nintendo games the

> "The very popularity of the NES fueled more demand and enticed more game developers to write games . . . making the system yet more attractive."[15]
>
> —*Carl Shapiro and Hal R. Varian, coauthors of* Information Rules.

bizarre became commonplace: Talking stylized lizards (Yoshi) battled with anthropomorphic bombs with mustaches (Big Bob-omb), and portly plumbers sought to save the princess. Nintendo games—*Mario*, *Zelda*, *Adventure Island*, and the many more to come—were odd, zany, often surreal, and uniquely Nintendo.

Most of the early NES games were programmed as side-scrollers, in which parallel projection allowed players to move characters left to right across the screen. With the *Legend of Zelda* and *SimCity* in the 1980s, Nintendo also pioneered bird's-eye, or helicopter, view, giving gamers a new way to move around within games and freeing them from the monotonous left-to-right navigation.

The Rise of Sega

With such innovations Nintendo was clearly the company to beat. Japanese competitor Sega, a veteran in the US arcade market, was among the rivals willing to try. Sega introduced its Master System in 1985 but made only the narrowest of profits due to Nintendo's domination of the important US and Japanese markets. Undaunted, Sega attempted to break Nintendo's hold once more with the Genesis system featuring a near-perfect console version of Sega's arcade hit *Altered Beast*, a "brawler" or "beat 'em up" platform game set in Ancient Greece in which a centurion is resurrected by the god Zeus to rescue his daughter Athena.

Sega also introduced new types of games to the US market. *NFL Sports Talk Football '93*, for instance, ushered in a new trend: the licensed sports game. *Sports Talk Football '93* featured star NFL player Joe Montana and all twenty-eight teams from the 1992–1993 season; additional players were added in future years. For the first time, users could manipulate their favorite players and teams in increasingly realistic competition, complete with play-by-play commentary. Michael Katz, former president of Sega of America writes, "The success of the Genesis . . . came from us having the 'personality' licensing position for software. . . . We COULD NOT compete with the strength of . . . Nintendo . . . so we decided to get personalities."[16] Within a year the sports franchise titles with spokesperson athletes were topsellers: *NBA Jam* sold almost 2 million and *NFL Football '94* sold over 1 million copies.

The Evolution of Game Control

From the earliest video games, the challenge of translating a player's intention into action has been one of the industry's greatest obstacles. Myriad designs have emerged—from the ingenious to the ridiculous—and many have failed because they were either too complex or too simple. Higinbotham's *Tennis for Two* was controlled with just a dial and button. *Spacewar!* had four switches that could turn the competing spaceships and thrust them forward. Accurate and intuitive motion was difficult using these switches. Atari's 1977 digital joystick had similar issues, lacking degrees of control for more complex or subtle game play.

Nintendo was the first to come up with the simple and now familiar cross-shaped directional pad ("D-pad"), which placed direction under one thumb and freed the other hand to control other buttons. First used for the handheld Donkey Kong game in 1982, it soon became the industry standard. Most modern controllers evolved from this model, becoming more ergonomic and adding trigger buttons for the index and middle fingers. Over time the joystick has also been rehabilitated and miniaturized to create additional controls for the thumbs. In 2006, however, Nintendo simultaneously revolutionized and simplified game control with the Wii Remote Controller. Combining a conventional controller with an infrared device to measure a player's movement relative to the infrared source, Nintendo commercialized motion-sensitive control and liberated players from the armchair while not saddling them with increasingly complex controllers.

As always, innovation was critical to success. Sega pioneered new ways to represent moving three-dimensional objects and characters on screen to give the impression of three dimensions without having to create a moving 3-D background. In Sega's *Sonic the Hedgehog*, for example, 3-D characters move through a two-dimensional platform, providing the illusion of greater depth without requiring extensive design work, greater storage capacity, or processing power. Through a combination of technological superiority, the introduction of console versions of popular arcade games, competitive pricing, and a highly effective marketing campaign based around the tagline "Genesis does what Nintendon't,"[17] Sega gradually lured market share away from NES.

Sega and Nintendo Battle It Out

The competition generated by the precipitous rise of Sega and Nintendo meant that home consoles were finally competing with the arcade technologically. New graphics chips, essentially used as dedicated graphics processors, manipulated images more efficiently and more rapidly. These allowed home consoles to reproduce the art styles of popular arcade games, featuring increasingly lavish backgrounds, broader color palettes, and graphical textures that gave the illusion of greater depth and more realistic visual effects.

While Nintendo dominated Japan, Sega reigned supreme in Europe. In the United States, the two came head to head. In addition to spurring new and ever better technologies, this competition prompted one of the most important developments for video game consoles: variety. In a quest to entice new players, Sega and Nintendo produced a vast number of exclusive games that could be played only on their respective consoles. Developers at each of the companies programmed games that capitalized on the strengths of its consoles and technologies. With a faster CPU, Sega's games moved noticeably quicker than Nintendo's. Nintendo, on the other hand, capitalized on superior graphics and sound, best demonstrated in the stunning colors and sharper images of *Star Fox* and the spellbinding audio effects of the *Thunder Force* series.

Compact Discs and CD-ROMs

In the 1980s compact discs (CDs) brought a new technology to the world of consoles. Philips and Sony had pioneered the technology and collaborated to produce a standard format and player technology. Music CDs hit the market in 1982; CD-ROMs, which used the same technology to store data, were released in 1985. Due to their vastly superior storage capability, CD-ROMs soon replaced cartridges in

The competition between titans Sega and Nintendo pushed the boundaries of technology in home gaming consoles. Nintendo capitalized on superior graphics and sound, best demonstrated by Star Fox.

the video game industry and helped usher in a new era of gaming. Whereas the best game cartridges could contain just 96 megabytes (MB) of data, a CD-ROM held upward of 680 MB. (A byte comprises 8 bits and a megabyte is 1,000 bytes.) Although CD technology initially was expensive, the price dropped precipitously, and within a few years CDs proved far cheaper than cartridges to manufacture and to distribute.

The technology led to a mad scramble by console companies to integrate CD technology into the gaming world. The superior data storage of CDs—combined with contemporary improvements in processing power and graphics chips—gave developers the option to incorporate three-dimensional graphics, cinematic cutscenes, pre-recorded soundtracks, and voice acting. Early techniques included "fixed 3D," in which three-dimensional foreground objects (such as game characters) were rendered in real time against a static background to display a high level of detail on minimal hardware (by today's standards). The new technology made serious storytelling possible.

The PlayStation

Nintendo partnered with Sony to design a CD drive for the Super Nintendo Entertainment System, which Nintendo introduced in the early 1990s. When Nintendo executives realized how much control Sony wanted, they backed out of the deal, leaving Sony to enter the market on its own terms. The result—the PlayStation—would rival any console on the market.

Built from the outset as a 3-D, CD-based system, the PlayStation won over consumers with graphics that Kutter Calloway, a professor at Fuller Theological Seminary calls "previously unimaginable."[18] Within five years and nine months Sony announced that more than 100 million units had been sold, "breaking the record as the fastest computer entertainment platform to reach this remarkable figure."[19] Sony's success was due in large part to its willingness to break from the conventions of other consoles. Among the most important innovations was a more complex game controller that provided greater control over game elements, enabled more intricate games, and therefore simply made games more fun to play.

Perhaps equally important, the PlayStation won over third-party programmers. Sony provided programmers with an accessible programming platform, allowing programmers to understand and access more fully the graphic, audio, and processing capabilities of the PlayStation and the parameters within which a game could be designed. This unprecedented access resulted in a substantial library of third-party games for the PlayStation. Sony's forward thinking would put PlayStation's games ahead of the competition for at least a decade.

Big Games Mean Big Business

Sega's attempts to keep up with console developments were largely unsuccessful. In the mid-1990s, Sega introduced the Saturn. Sales of the console met expectations in Japan, due largely to the popularity of the games, but the console flopped in the US market. Sales of the Saturn's successor, the Dreamcast, were even more dismal, and Sega dropped out of the console market to focus almost exclusively on game development.

This left just three players in the console market: electronics giant Sony; veteran video game producer Nintendo; and a new contender, the PC giant Microsoft. Sony continued to demonstrate its ability to compete with the PlayStation 2, which was the first console to play

Sony's PlayStation 2 was the first console to play DVDs, which effectively quintupled the capacity of CDs. This facilitated longer and more visually appealing games. Between 2000 and 2013, 155 million PlayStation 2s were sold.

DVDs. DVD technology effectively quintupled the capacity of CDs and facilitated longer, more visually appealing games. Between 2000 and 2013, 155 million PlayStation 2s were sold, making it the best-selling home console ever.

Nintendo countered with a new console of its own: the Game-Cube. This was the first Nintendo console to use digital discs instead of cartridges, but it did not play DVDs. Nintendo also offered up the Game Boy Player, a peripheral adaptor that allowed the games designed for the Game Boy (a handheld device that Nintendo had released in 1989) to be played on the GameCube. This increased the GameCube's appeal, but many classified it as a kids' toy due to the unsophisticated plastic design and the fact that there were relatively few adult-oriented games for the device.

The first American company to take part in the console market since Atari, Microsoft entered the competition relatively late, with the release of the Xbox in 2001. But Microsoft's roots in personal computing changed the industry. The Xbox brought with it a host of features borrowed from the PC world: a hard drive to save games; an ethernet port for broadband Internet access; and Xbox LIVE, which allowed online and interactive gaming. PC developers flocked to create games for the console, and these games cemented Xbox's popularity, particularly among older teens and adults. Among the games developed for the Xbox was *Halo*, a first-person shooter game that combined eerily realistic graphics, intense game play, and a well-structured storyline. *Halo* would become one of the most successful video game franchises in history.

The Wii

Having cornered a significant part of the kid's video game market with the GameCube, Nintendo sought to attract a broader market. Nintendo president Satoru Iwata pushed his developers to find new ways to use existing technology—a design philosophy that Gunpei Yokoi, the Nintendo genius responsible for the Game Boy and several of Nintendo's other best-sellers, referred to as "lateral thinking with withered technology."[20] By *withered* technology (sometimes translated as "seasoned"), Yokoi meant the technology that was old and therefore cheap and well understood. He believed that success in the gaming world did not require cutting-edge technology: what it required instead was finding new, fun, and exciting ways to use existing technology differently.

Believing that the industry was shortsighted in focusing on core gamers, Iwata announced in 2006 his intention to take a different path: "For some time, we have believed the game industry is ready for disruption. Not just from Nintendo, but from all game developers. It is what we all need to expand our audience. It is what we all need to expand our imaginations."[21] Nintendo believed the console market was already saturated. Rather than compete with increasingly more power, the Nintendo design team focused on the other aspects of game play. "We started with the idea that we wanted to come up with a unique game interface," explains Shigeru Miyamoto. "The consensus was that power isn't everything for a console. Too many powerful consoles can't coexist. It's like having only ferocious dinosaurs. They might fight and hasten their own extinction."[22]

> "For some time, we have believed the game industry is ready for disruption. . . . It is what we all need to expand our audience. It is what we all need to expand our imaginations."[21]
>
> —Satoru Iwata, president of Nintendo.

After almost five years of development, the Nintendo launched its Wii in 2006. Technologically, the Nintendo Wii was inferior to its competitors: It had neither a hard drive nor high-definition graphics. But the Wii Remote introduced an innovative, intuitive, motion-sensing game control. Working much like a television's remote controller, the Wii Remote used an infrared system to determine a player's orientation, position, and movement. The system allowed a host of motion-dependent applications. The earliest Wii games encouraged players to get off the couch to dance, play tennis, bowl, or perform other movements—countering criticisms that video games made "couch potatoes" out of teens. "Our goal was to come up with a machine that moms would want—easy to use, quick to start up, not a huge energy drain, and quiet while it was running," says Miyamoto. Nintendo also created the Wii to play older Nintendo games because "moms would hate it if they had to have several consoles lying around."[23]

The Consoles of Today

Today new, improved versions of Sony's PlayStation, Microsoft's Xbox, and Nintendo's Wii continue to dominate the video game console market, as each has built on the innovations of the others to continue to improve the home gaming experience. To compete with the Wii, for instance, Sony and Microsoft have come out with their own motion-sensing systems, controllers, and games. Video games also have incorporated new types of peripherals into the games, including everything from skateboards to the range of musical instruments that have made the *Rock Band* series a bestseller.

With the growing affordability of powerful PCs, laptops, smartphones, and tablets, many have predicted the demise of gaming consoles. "The bastion of video games—the game console—should be dead. Or at least dying," writes Greg Perrault in a 2014 blog.

> "The bastion of video games—the game console— should be dead. Or at least dying."[24]
>
> —Greg Perrault, media researcher at the University of Missouri.

"Digital, streaming, cross-platform content seems to be the name of the game. But when Microsoft introduced the Xbox One video console earlier this year and espoused such a digital plan, it led to a tremendous backlash. Microsoft did a complete 180 turn in order to address the desires of their customer base."[24] Microsoft had intended to require Xbox One owners to connect to the Internet once a day— a move intended not only to prevent game piracy but also to allow game publishers more control over access, resale, and fees. Consumer complaints (before the Xbox One was even released) led the company to reverse this policy. In 2014 Sony and Microsoft released the PlayStation 4 and Xbox One, respectively: Each sold more than one million units in just 24 hours.

Innovation and investment have made the video game console a fixture in living rooms throughout the world. According to the Entertainment Software Association, more than half of US households have at least one device, and most of these have two or more. Furthermore, more people play games on their console (68 percent) than any other device. Given the popularity of dance and sports titles, console-driven active video games may someday replace TV time as the family entertainment of choice.

In the Palm of Your Hand

Chapter Three

Just as video games emerged in accordance with computer technology, it was the electronic calculator that gave rise to the handheld game. The early state-of-the-art calculators were bulky and extremely expensive. In 1966 a calculator cost more than $1,000 ($5,500 in today's money). The best of these desktop behemoths displayed thirteen digits and performed only the most basic mathematical functions of addition, subtraction, multiplication, and division. Microprocessor technology brought the electronic calculator off the desk and into the hand. As this technology became cheaper and more accessible, it contributed to the rise of a new form of entertainment: the handheld electronic video game.

The Mattel toy company was among the first companies to exploit the potential of microprocessor technology for the game industry. Michael Katz issued the design team a challenge to "come up with a game that was electronic that was the same size as a calculator."[25] *Mattel Auto Race* and *Mattel Football*, both released in 1976, were the first in line.

Compared to what would come later, *Mattel Auto Race* and *Mattel Football* were extremely basic. Essentially, these repurposed standard calculator hardware as an electronic game. Rudimentary dashes made from bright LED lights represented both the player's character icon—either a car or a running back—as well as the obstacles that attempted to stop the player's forward progression across the screen. The player used a side-to-side switch to change the car's lanes or the quarterback's position to maneuver past the obstacles before time ran out. The accompanying sound effects consisted of simple beeps.

Mattel's handheld games met with immediate success and almost single-handedly launched the handheld game industry, turning it into a $400 million market practically overnight. Within two years veteran game makers Milton Bradley and Parker Brothers had their own handheld electronic games. Soon, Coleco, Entex, Bandai, and a host of other manufacturers joined in, often creating miniature versions of popular arcade games.

As with other game media, companies sought to increase market share by improving the gaming experience. With the release of the Microvision in 1979, Milton Bradley became the first company to provide a handheld option with interchangeable game cartridges. But the Microvision's tiny screen limited the types of games it could display clearly, and it was plagued by mechanical failures. As a result of these limitations, it lasted in the marketplace for less than five years, but it had given gamers a glimpse of the future.

One of the biggest challenges for handheld games was how to pack a powerful battery in such a small package. In 1982 Bandai became the first to solve the problem with the *LCD Solarpower*, which supplemented battery power with solar panels and also featured two layered LCD panels to create a 3D effect. Another innovation was housing the unit in a now familiar clamshell-like hinged case.

Watch Nintendo Change the Game

Meanwhile, Gunpei Yokoi was on a train during his commute home when he saw a businessman playing with an LCD calculator. Always curious, Yokoi began to wonder whether there was a market for handheld games that could entertain adults on their commutes. He devised a small, portable, rectangular device that could play a single game while also serving as a clock (with alarm). In 1980 Nintendo came out with the first in its *Game & Watch* line, a series of products that had a digital time display in the corner of the screen and buttons to control on-screen characters. Later models incorporated a cross-shaped directional pad (D-pad) for more movement options. Yokoi's D-pad would become a staple of many video game controllers and later would earn an Emmy Award in Technology & Engineering.

The Japanese market embraced *Game & Watch*, spurring the creation of a host of games and titles. But the series made fewer inroads in United States. Consequently, Yokoi and his team set to work marrying the elements of handheld LCD devices to the NES console to create a small device that might capture the lucrative US market. The result was the Nintendo Game Boy, which Nintendo released in Japan in April 1989 and to the North American market a few months later.

Released in 1989, the original Nintendo Game Boy (pictured) was panned by industry critics for its small screen, monochrome graphics, and minimal processing power. However, these features enabled a small battery and low price, which made the Game Boy highly attractive to consumers.

Industry critics were appalled by the substandard specifications of the Game Boy, complaining of its monochrome graphical display, small screen, and inadequate processing power. But these same elements were what made the Game Boy a success: Nintendo had compromised on design to keep the price low and the battery small. The

The Rapid Rise of *Minecraft*

While many of the top-selling games of all time—*Super Mario, Mario Kart, Grand Theft Auto, Halo*—have been around for a decade or longer, *Minecraft* rose to the top in just a few years. *Minecraft* was released in its alpha (untested) state in 2009 by Swedish programmer Markus Persson. After several upgrades and updates, the full release version was published on November 18, 2011. Testifying to the popularity of mobile game playing, Android and Apple iOS versions of *Minecraft* were released before the PC version. An Xbox version of the game was released in May 2012. More than 35 million copies of the game have been sold across all platforms.

Minecraft's appeal is due to its range of play. The world of *Minecraft* is divided into biomes, such as deserts, ice-capped mountains, or jungles. Within these biomes, players walk, jump, or otherwise move across a procedurally generated surface, encountering various terrain, animals, and villagers as they go. The *Minecraft* website explains that the game can be about creating "wonderful, imaginative things. It can also be about adventuring with friends or watching the sun rise over a blocky ocean. It's pretty. Brave players battle terrible things in The Nether, which is more scary than pretty. You can also visit a land of mushrooms if it sounds more like your cup of tea." The variety appeals to gamers of all demographics and keeps players coming back again and again—the main keys to success in the video game world.

Quoted in "Home" on Minecraft website, https://minecraft.net.

Game Boy's popularity was cemented by the inspired inclusion of *Tetris*, an extremely popular tile-matching puzzle game designed in the Soviet Union. Nintendo had intended to include a Mario game with the Game Boy, but video game entrepreneur Henk Rogers sold the president of Nintendo's America division on *Tetris*: "If you want boys to play, include Mario," he said. "If you want everyone to play— mothers, fathers, brothers, sisters—include Tetris."[26] Mario and several other games would be available on the launch date, but it was the highly addictive *Tetris* that would come bundled in the box.

The gamble paid off. Within the first two weeks of its release in Japan, the entire stock of three hundred thousand units was sold; in the United States forty thousand Game Boy units were sold on the first day. Industry expert Travis Fahs writes, "While Nintendo fought tooth and nail to get the NES onto the shelves of stores and into the minds of American kids, the Game Boy was an overnight success."[27] To validate Rogers's point, more than 40 percent of the units were purchased by women or girls.

The release of the Game Boy inspired numerous imitations and contenders. Atari's Lynx, for instance, came out just a few months after the Game Boy. Although it offered better graphics and sound than the Game Boy and was introduced with a range of new games, the Lynx's high price tag put it out of the running. Daniel Sloan notes in his seminal work *Playing to Wiin*, "Game Boy bowled over technologically superior handheld offerings from competitors, such as Atari and Sega, with [Gunpei] Yokoi's vision of affordable fun going for under $50. Its 2.6-inch display, a 160x144 pixel LCD screen . . . could run for 30 hours on two AA batteries."[28]

The Game Boy also benefited from the fact that it was designed to be able to use the entire Nintendo library, which numbered more than seven hundred titles.

> "Game Boy bowled over technologically superior handheld offerings from competitors, such as Atari and Sega, with [Gunpei] Yokoi's vision of affordable fun going for under $50."[28]
>
> —Daniel Sloan, author of Playing to Wiin.

Game Boy Gets a Makeover

Nintendo's Game Boy reigned supreme for nearly a decade. But a decade was a long time in the rapidly changing world of gaming, and game developers and consumers clamored for something new. In 1998 Nintendo responded with the Game Boy Color.

The Game Boy Color featured a color screen that was capable of displaying up to fifty-six colors simultaneously, instead of its predecessor's four shades of gray. The processor was twice as fast as the original Game Boy's with double the memory, allowing longer game play and more detailed graphics. The Game Boy Color also featured an infrared communications port for wireless linking.

The Game Boy Color also introduced a new element to handheld video games: backward compatibility. This means that a new device can still play the game cartridges of its predecessors. In the case of Game Boy Color, any of the games developed for the original Game Boy could be played on the new system. It was this backward compatibility that made the Game Boy Color a commercial success. But despite this success and its continued primacy in the handheld games market, it was evident that Nintendo was merely repackaging an aging product. Jeff Ryan, who wrote a book about the Nintendo empire, notes, "The word 'withered' was . . . apt for the Game Boy Color. . . . It was a legacy machine, surviving (and thriving) because few wanted to discard all the *Dr. Mario* and *Pokémon* cartridges they had amassed over the years."[29]

> "The Game Boy Color . . . was a legacy machine, surviving (and thriving) because few wanted to discard all the *Dr. Mario* and *Pokémon* cartridges they had amassed over the years."[29]
>
> —*Jeff Ryan, author of* Super Mario: How Nintendo Conquered America.

Building on its success and the lion's share of the market, Nintendo released in 2001 the Game Boy Advance, which added two shoulder buttons on the edges of the device, a larger screen, and more computing power to the Game Boy Color. Two years later the Game Boy Advance SP offered a more compact, clamshell design, with a front-lit color display and rechargeable battery. In conjunction with the GameCube, the release of the Game Boy Advance also introduced cross-selling connectivity, as the handheld device could be used as a console controller for a number of Game-Cube games. But the true genius behind the Game Boy Advance series was related to the games: Rather than produce a few new games for the unit, Nintendo retooled and repackaged games it already had in its huge library. The strategy assumed that every few years a new generation of children would receive a Game Boy as a gift; because that generation had never played any of the old Mario games, for example, the Advance versions of the games would seem brand new. In one fell swoop, Nintendo created an awe-inspiring library of "new" games that could be sold cheaply because no significant development or programming was needed. "Every game from 1990 on could have a second life, a paperback release, on the Game Boy

Advance,"[30] writes Ryan. Nintendo once again had found a way to corner the market.

The Nintendo DS

As if to prove that it could outdo itself, Nintendo reinforced its supremacy in the handheld device market with the 2004 release of the Nintendo DS. The DS was a portable gaming package in a hinged case with two screens, the lower of which was touch sensitive. Included with the DS was a stylus, which got mixed reviews. Some early adopters found the stylus—which one reviewer called a "short plastic toothpick" gimmicky and clumsy to use.[31]

The naysayers could not have been more wrong: both initial and ongoing sales of the DS far exceeded expectations. What set the DS apart was its target demographic. Again, Nintendo had designed with the family in mind. Nintendo's Shigeru Miyamoto remarked in an interview with *Businessweek*, "Most people think video games are all about a child staring at a TV with a joystick in his hands. I don't. They should belong to the entire family. I want families to play video games together."[32] The DS came in several different colors, including pink. This feature, and girl-friendly games such as *Nintendogs*, *Super Princess Peach*, and *Yoshi Touch & Go*, helped Nintendo corner the market on female gamers.

Sony Plays Catch-Up

Would-be competitors continued to be hampered by costs. Among the best of these products was Sony's PlayStation Portable (PSP), which was released in Japan in December 2004 and in North America in March 2005. The PSP was the first handheld video game console to use an optical disc format—the Universal Media Disc (UMD)—as its primary storage medium. The UMD could hold up to 1.8 gigabytes of data, enabling the playing of sophisticated games and full-length feature films. The PSP also offered a large viewing screen and connectivity with the PlayStation 2 and 3, other PSPs, and the Internet. The technology of the PSP was far more advanced than anything Nintendo offered, and it had some of the best initial games ever released, including *Spider-Man*, *Need for Speed*, and *Twisted Metal*.

In response to the huge success of Nintendo's Game Boy, Sony developed the PlayStation Portable (pictured) known as the PSP. It had superior storage space and could play sophisticated games and movies. But it was nearly twice the price of other handheld models.

Author and gamer Joel Durham Jr. writes, "The PSP was designed to be a truly high-performance gaming powerhouse, complete with graphics that rival those of the legendary PlayStation 2, audio that sounds more realistic than the dog barking next door, and controls that are incredibly innovative for a portable gaming system."[33] The PSP had one significant flaw, however: It was pricey. The Nintendo DS retailed for under $150, the PSP $245.

Nintendo appreciated the need to continue to innovate, however. In 2006 and 2009 it released sleeker, cheaper, and slightly improved-upon versions of its DS. Then in 2011 it took the technology to a new dimension: 3-D. With Nintendo's signature backward compatibility, the 3DS also featured an online service called the Nintendo eShop, which allowed it to compete with the ready availability of games made for the growing smartphone market.

Tapping into Telephone Technology

Nintendo would not find its strongest competition from other gaming technologies but rather from the world of digital telephone. The potential of cellular phones as gaming platforms was first seen in the mid-1990s, when such phones became small and cheap enough for the mass market. Designers quickly realized that better processors would enable cellular phones to do more than take calls; they could be used as entertainment devices—a portable means to play games and, later, music and movies. The game *Snake*, a rudimentary game that first appeared in 1997 on the Nokia 6110 as pixelated black squares moving on a green background, was an instant hit. That same year Wireless Application Protocol (WAP) enabled mobile devices to connect to the Internet. Combined with the increasing affordability of handsets, WAP technology contributed to a revolution in mobile gaming. "The global trend towards mobile gaming . . . occurred in partnership with the transformation of mobile phones from communication devices to multimedia devices par excellence,"[34] notes video game expert Larissa Hjorth.

Nokia was among the first to recognize the promise. In 2003 it introduced a combination MP3 player, cellphone, personal digital assistant (PDA), radio, and gaming device called the N-Gage. Although the market was ready for this type of system, the N-Gage fell short of expectations. The vertically oriented screen made too many games difficult to play. Other layout defects included the fact that the battery had to be removed to change game cartridges. Ikka Raiskinen, director of the entertainment and media business at Nokia, readily acknowledged some of these defects but thought the comparison to traditional gaming platforms was unjust. "The critical feedback [is coming] from hardcore gamers," Raiskinen explains. "They compare the N-Gage experience with the game experience on the consoles. From that perspective, they're certainly right. But to us, N-Gage is about mobile online gaming. It's not the device, but content and games that count."[35]

Apple fared far better. Its iPhone 3G and the launch of the Apple App Store in 2008 forever changed not only how people used mobile phones but also how they perceived the technology. The App Store,

> "The global trend towards mobile gaming . . . occurred in partnership with the transformation of mobile phones from communication devices to multimedia devices par excellence."[34]
>
> —Larissa Hjorth, deputy dean of Media and Communication and professor of the Games Program at RMIT University.

47

There's an App for That!

On July 10, 2008, Apple's App Store was launched via an update to iTunes. The next day the iPhone 3G was released, pre-loaded with App Store support. The App Store was an immediate hit: By early 2011 the App Store had had over 10 billion downloads and by July of that year had exceeded 15 billion. In 2013 that number hit 40 billion. The store was a treasure trove for third-party app developers inspired both by the ease of use and the highly accessible revenue streams. The success of Apple's App Store led to the launch of similar services by competitors, including Google and Amazon. By 2010 the term "app" was awarded the honor of being "Word of the Year" by the American Dialect Society. Accessible from any iPhone, iPod Touch, and iPad, the Apple App Store soon became the only way to directly download Apple applications onto any Apple iOS device. Yet while Apple's apps were first to market, Android app stores now account for over 80 percent of the app market. Mobile apps serve a wide variety of purposes, but more than half of all apps that are downloaded today are games.

which was the first application store operated directly by a mobile platform, provided unprecedented and easy access to new applications (apps) for iPhones and other Apple products. The iPhone was designed to do far more than what a traditional cell phone did; users could listen to music, for example, or even play full-length video games.

As Apple cornered the market on the smartphone industry, it built on its success with the iPad. This first "tablet" was essentially a portable computer that enabled the user to shoot video, take photos, play music, surf the web, and perform a host of other functions. It also was perhaps a perfect platform for the latest mobile video game apps. Other mobile phone manufacturers, meanwhile, got in on the action, embracing the Android operating system and creating similar online stores where the latest applications could be downloaded.

Games on the Run

Lightweight, portable, and always on hand, mobile phones were a natural fit for gaming. Within just a few years, more than half of all the apps downloaded onto mobile phones were games. By 2009 the games market annual value was estimated at between $7 billion and $30 billion; by 2012 it exceeded $66 billion. Indeed, within the video game industry mobile games represented the fastest-growing market segment, with an average annual growth rate of 19 percent for smartphones and 48 percent for tablets.

Manufacturers reaped in the benefits of the new technology. For the video game industry, mobile devices offered versatility. Mobile games required much shorter lead times and were exponentially cheaper to market. The limited memory of mobile phones meant smaller and therefore more quickly produced games, and the consolidated App Store marketplace reduced advertising and marketing costs enormously.

The advent of mobile gaming to some extent mitigated the relentless expansion of video games. Shorter, more easily controlled games—so-called casual games—became increasingly popular, taking in a larger target audience than the existing console game market. The games available as apps varied widely in terms of sophistication, genre, and type. What they had in common was ease of use, due to the devices' touch screens and intuitive controls. The most successful games, as always, were extremely easy to learn and almost impossible to master: a combination that makes them addictive to even the most casual user.

> "N-Gage is about mobile online gaming. It's not the device, but content and games that count."[35]
>
> —Ikka Raiskinen, director of entertainment and media at Nokia.

Video Games Break Out of the Box

Chapter Four

The story of video games has consistently been one of using technology to overcome the obstacles that are inherent in a technology-driven product. But only in the field of online gaming has technology rather than economics truly driven the pace of change. Owing to the inherent flexibility and constant technological improvement of online platforms, online gaming has been at the forefront of innovation since the earliest years of video games. In recent years video game companies and developers have finally seen the commercial potential of these platforms and have turned once again to revolutionary technologies, embracing platforms such as the cloud, social media, and sophisticated virtual reality constructs.

The rise of the Internet and online gaming are an integral part of this story. Although no one anticipated the use of the Internet for gaming—or for many of the other purposes for which it is used today—most gamers cannot imagine life without it. The multiplayer game played over the Internet is as integral to the marketing of video gaming today as the joystick was to the earliest console games.

Online gaming has moved in two distinctly different directions, each with its own distinct audience and development agenda, and each gaining in popularity. Game developers have responded in kind. Whereas the core gamer community has reveled in the increasingly immersive, realistic, and complex game play and virtual worlds, a casual gaming audience has responded exponentially well to increasingly compelling social networking games: relatively short, easily accessible games with clearly defined goals and rewards for keeping the game going.

Online game innovation has been driven primarily by the game developers themselves, often working solo or in pairs with little support. Andrew Kirmse, who created one of the first multiplayer online games, details the difficulty of trying to launch *Meridian 59* in the 1990s: "Our early testers were very enthusiastic despite the lack of game play and the presence of numerous crippling bugs. We entered a period of intense development, coming out with new versions every 3–4 weeks. . . . The game's artwork, in particular, suffered from poor organization and management, though we were all feeling the stress from trying to produce new features, test existing ones, and run customer support."[36]

The Rise of LAN-Based Games

Some of the technologies that have allowed for the latest breakthroughs in video gaming have been around for a long time—at least by video game standards. In the 1970s the rise of packet-based computer networking technology (a digital networking method which groups transmitted data, regardless of content, type, or structure, into suitably sized blocks or "packets") facilitated new types of computer networks, notably local area networks (LANs) and wide area networks (WANs)—the most sophisticated of which became the Internet. The spread of LANs and WANs to facilitate file sharing and communication also gave rise to network gaming, as users in geographically dispersed locations could play games with one another.

The earliest LAN-based games were incidental, if not accidental. In 1972 the University of Illinois pioneered the PLATO IV terminal as part of a time-sharing system for computer-aided learning. The intention was to offer coursework to students, local schools, and other universities, but PLATO soon also gave rise to students who wanted to create multiplayer games. By 1978 the system was teeming with multiplayer interactive graphical games, including dungeon fantasy games such as *Rogue*, combat games such as *Airfight*, and space games such as *Empire* and *Spasim*. Each of these early PLATO-based games enabled inter-player messaging and play for thirty-two simultaneous users.

As with most video game advances, Internet/LAN-based game play did not take off right away. The technology was versatile, but it was also expensive. The vast majority of early LAN-based games were at universities. One of the most popular was the Multi-User Dungeon, or what most people simply called a MUD. This multiplayer virtual world sought to replicate aspects of the eminently popular role-playing board game *Dungeons & Dragons* while incorporating new elements such as online chat. MUDs had significant influence in the development of so-called "massively multiplayer online role-playing games," or MMORPGs.

In 1984, at the nadir of the home console industry, two students from the Mines Paris Tech (officially the École Nationale Supérieure des Mines de Paris) in France developed and operated a global MUD that they called Multi Access Dungeon (MAD) on BITNET, a cooperative network used mainly by universities. Initially consisting of one and then several multistory labyrinths populated by monsters or robots, MAD also allowed player avatars (in-game characters that explore the world at the direction of the user) to communicate with one another. News of MAD spread rapidly by word of mouth, and soon a significant number of BITNET systems were playing on the MAD terminal, overwhelming BITNET on several occasions. In 1986, alarmed by the game's runaway popularity, BITNET administrators banned the game, but the experience had revealed something very interesting. "With the arrival of real-time strategy, we discovered that our greatest opponent might be the person sitting next to us," notes Craig Detweiler, author of a 2010 book on video games. "Tournaments and online gaming exploded with the opportunity to play live, sophisticated competition against anyone, anytime, anywhere, worldwide. Video games became a global contest."[37]

> "Tournaments and online gaming exploded with the opportunity to play live, sophisticated competition against anyone, anytime, anywhere, worldwide. Video games became a global contest."[37]
>
> —Craig Detweiler, author of Halos and Avatars: Playing Video Games with God.

True peer-to-peer (or computer-to-computer) online games had an unlikely origin: a high school student. Greg Thompson wrote *Maze War* in 1973 during his summer as an intern at NASA's Ames Research Center in California. When he went to college at MIT that fall, he took a copy of the program with him, writing a server version that allowed up to eight computers to play against each other. MIT's computers were connected to a WAN, the newly minted ARPANET. Consequently, computers at other ARPANET sites could also play. The first-person shooter game—among the first of this genre—became immensely popular. (First-person shooter games enable the

At the 40th annual Gen Con convention, gamers review their strategies while playing the eminently popular role-playing board game Dungeons & Dragons. Popular and early online video games called Multi-User Dungeons (MUDs) sought to replicate aspects of the role-playing game.

player to take on the perspective of the player in the game and usually involve shooting something at enemy characters while trying to achieve a predetermined goal.) In 1977 a staff member at Xerox's Palo Alto Research Center rewrote the game to be played on the Xerox Ethernet network. In 1986 *Maze War* was made available for Unix workstations across the modern Internet, making *Maze War* the first Internet game.

Multiplayer games brought new forms of game play and, many people felt, more fun. John Taylor, who created *Island of Kesmai* with University of Virginia classmate Kelton Flinn, later said, "We were always more interested in multiplayer games than any other kind. When you play against a computer, eventually you begin to anticipate its moves. A person, on the other hand, is never completely predictable."[38]

Profits and Pay

These earliest multiplayer games were free to players, but network administrators were trying to figure out how to recoup their costs for hosting the apparatus on which they were played. In 1984 CompuServe, one of the largest Internet service providers, introduced as part of its service *Island of Kesmai*, making it the first commercial multiplayer online role-playing game. *Island of Kesmai* borrowed features of game play from the earlier *Rogue* and other *Dungeons & Dragons*–style games. One of the other notable features of the *Island of Kesmai* game was the quest-based reward system: players completed a mission in return for rewards. This feature would be heavily used in the subsequent popular multiplayer games such as *World of Warcraft* and *Runescape*. But the most innovative feature of the game was its multiplayer aspect. Gamer Justin Olivetti writes in a review of *Island of Kesmai*: "Both solo and grouping was possible, although it was definitely difficult to progress without the help of a friend or two. While *Dungeons of Kesmai* [*Island of Kesmai's* predecessor] could only host six players at a time, *Island of Kesmai* expanded that to a then-mindblowing 100 players traipsing around the game world."[39]

Island of Kesmai was included as part of the CompuServe subscription package, but players were charged the connection fee, which at the time was six dollars per hour for a 300-baud modem and twelve dollars per hour for a 1200-baud modem. (For dial-up modems, the baud rate denoted the number of pulses per second the modem could send or receive, which at the time equated to the number of bits that would be sent per second.) With *Island of Kesmai*, online gaming was an option, but the rates precluded it from becoming truly affordable entertainment.

Other companies followed CompuServe's lead. In 1986 Lucasfilm Games introduced *Habitat* as an online game for the Commodore 64 home computer, enabling users—or rather, their onscreen avatars—to meet in an online virtual community. *Habitat* was followed by *Club Caribe*, a revolutionary world that allowed players to wander around an entire island collecting tokens and interacting directly with other players.

Virtual Goods in the Real World

With the rise of MMORPGs and social networking games, many companies have emerged seeking to sell virtual goods and associated services within the games. This practice—amassing gold or other in-game items for financial profit—is frequently described as "gold farming." And it is big business. Edward Castronova, an associate professor in the Department of Telecommunications at Indiana University notes, "Where there's money to be made, there will be people out to make it. Where some gamers are playing for fun, others are pursuing a new kind of day-trading game."

After *World of Warcraft* producer Blizzard started offering free trial accounts, for instance, players noticed an increase in unwanted messages from automated game accounts (called "bots") advertising goods and services. As in real financial markets, not all currency was the same: gold was fourteen times more expensive in US realms than in their European counterparts.

Game producers have tried to put an end to such commercialism. Game rules typically specify that items may not be bought or sold outside of the game, at risk of being suspended from play or forever banned from the game. In May 2007 Blizzard took its efforts one step further by filing a lawsuit against players trading against the rules in *World of Warcraft*. In February 2008 the players agreed to refrain from using any *World of Warcraft* chat or communication for such purposes. The practice of trading gold has continued to be controversial in and beyond the *World of Warcraft*, however, representing just one of the many complexities of the virtual world.

Edward Castronova, "Virtual Life Satisfaction," *Kyklos,* vol. 64, no. 3, 2011, p. 313.

The Virtual World Becomes Real

Although *Island of Kesmai*, *Habitat*, and *Club Caribe* are considered multiplayer games, their limitations preclude them from being categorized as massively multiplayer, or MMORPGs. In 1991 this honor went to *Neverwinter Nights*, another *Dungeons & Dragons* derivative that was released for users of America Online (AOL) at the cost of six dollars per hour. As the capacity for the game grew (from

50 players in 1991 to 500 in 1995), so did its popularity. (AOL eventually offered the game to subscribers free of charge.) By 1997, when *Neverwinter Nights* was discontinued, it had an estimated 115,000 players, with up to 2,000 playing at any one time.

In December 1995 games publisher 3DO decided to offer its MMORPG, *Meridian 59*, directly to consumers for a monthly subscription fee. It also brought 3-D functionality to the online virtual world, which allowed players to experience the game world through their characters' eyes. "We wanted the game to be . . . a medieval RPG [role-playing game], but with more player interaction," says Kirmse. *Meridian 59* broke new ground. "For many people using the Internet for the first time, Meridian was how people actually 'saw' people on the other end of their chat messages," explains Kirmse. "The game's character gesture, such as waving, added a personal feel to an impersonal network."[40] Many of the elements that made *Meridian 59* successful became standard in later games.

The next generation of MMORPGs included the medieval-themed game *Dark Age of Camelot*. Among its innovations was player-versus-player technology that enabled real-time interactive conflict, such as swordfights, between players. *Dark Age of Camelot* also forced players to select a realm (or team) and essentially play for that team during the game.

Lessons from Multiplayer Games

What MMORPGs have proved is that people not only like playing games but that they also like playing them together. "The idea of the 'lone gamer' is really not true anymore," says video game designer Jane McGonigal. "Up to 65 percent of gaming now is social, played either online or in the same room with people we know in real life."[41] Taken as a whole, multiplayer role-playing games changed the very nature of gaming by emphasizing inter-player interaction, cooperation, and teambuilding. In a GameSpy article on the history of *Dungeons & Dragons*, authors Allen Rausch and Miguel Lopez write of the 1991 online game *Neverwinter Nights*, "With hundreds of loyal players all adventuring in the same city . . . politics, guilds, and alliances quickly formed a social community that was far more important than the actual game."[42] Players might be able to advance on their own, but they usually could not get very far. And so avid players began to form allegiances with one another, sometimes finding themselves allied with people with whom they otherwise had little in common.

Game developers and companies were eager to capitalize on the new market, expanding the MMORPGs into new genres. But role-playing games, with their innate ability to suck players in, have remained the most promising for multiplayer gaming, regardless of the number of users. Nina Huntemann, an associate professor at Suffolk University, points out in her documentary *Game Over*, "What's really exciting about video games is you don't just interact with the game physically—you're not just moving your hand on a joystick, but you're asked to interact with the game psychologically and emotionally as well. You're not just watching the characters on screen; you're becoming those characters."[43]

> "With hundreds of loyal players all adventuring in the same city . . . politics, guilds, and alliances quickly formed a social community that was far more important than the actual game."[42]
>
> —Allen Rausch and Miguel Lopez, authors and experts on the history of Dungeons & Dragons.

World of Warcraft

Perhaps the most groundbreaking MMORPG is *World of Warcraft*, which, after five years in development, received universal acclaim upon its much-anticipated 2004 release. "World of Warcraft is a complex game whose complexity is carefully disguised by a simple, highly legible, uncluttered interface and an impressive 3D graphics engine, which delivers high performance on a wide range of systems while not skimping on pure flash," writes Greg Kasavin in a 2004 review for GameSpot. "The game's interface is so slick and easy to learn and understand, and the gameplay itself is so quickly intuitive, that there isn't even a tutorial to wade through." Like reviewers, users love *World of Warcraft* for intuitive game play and its rich graphics. "Here is the online role-playing game you should play, no matter who you are," advises Kasavin. "World of Warcraft brings out all the best aspects of this style of gaming, if not many of the best aspects of gaming in general. . . . Such high quality simply cannot be expected, nor should it be missed."[44]

Gamers play World of Warcraft (WoW) *at an exhibition stand during the Gamescom 2011 fair. Perhaps the most groundbreaking multiuser online game of all time,* WoW *was praised for a complexity that is disguised by a simple and easy-to-learn interface.*

Critics and users alike lauded the game's quickness, pointing out, for instance, that avatars who die are quickly revived, allowing players to be back enjoying the action at once. Thanks to the game's almost universal appeal, *World of Warcraft* had more than 7 million users by the end of the decade; in January 2014 Blizzard announced that more than 100 million *World of Warcraft* accounts had been created over the game's lifetime. It not only remains the most-subscribed MMORPG but also the highest-grossing video game of all time, making well over $10 billion.

Fantasy and Film

With the growth and proliferation of affordable broadband, significant competition arose from free-to-play MMORPGs that attracted a huge number of registered users. Among the pay-to-play MMORPGs, game developers focused on giving players visually stunning graphics, supported by higher-speed internet connections.

"Video games and films are starting to look more like each other," says novelist, playwright, screenwriter, and film director Adam Rapp. "The graphics are so spellbinding and real. People playing video games are like filmmakers—you can control the dream in your own living room. You create your own destiny; you become your own author."[45]

Many recent MMORPGs have emulated fantasy films: In 2007 *The Lord of the Rings Online: Shadows of Angmar* became one of the first to enjoy commercial success. Other new titles—*Age of Conan, Warhammer Online, Star Wars, Star Trek Online*—often sounded a lot like the line-up at the local theatre. In addition to capitalizing on the popularity of these movies, developers could also sometimes borrow visual elements and even storylines.

> "[W]hat's really exciting about video games is you don't just interact with the game physically—you're not just moving your hand on a joystick, but you're asked to interact with the game psychologically and emotionally as well."[43]
>
> —Nina Huntemann, associate professor of Media Studies at Suffolk University.

Developers also looked for crossover opportunities between mobile platforms and online gaming. In 2010 *Pocket Legends* became the first MMORPG to be released for iOS and Android devices. Despite the game's initial success, subscriptions tapered off almost immediately, leading to the suspension of the game in 2012.

Life in a Cloud

While the development of online gaming has in large part depended on important technological advances in the hardware on which games are played, the advent of "cloud gaming" made the capacity of a user's computer—and more recently, tablet—largely irrelevant. The cloud, which relies on servers connected through the Internet or other networks, was a seemingly natural progression for online gaming. Game servers could now run the processing needs of the games, allowing direct and on-demand streaming of games onto computers, consoles, and mobile devices, where user commands are transmitted directly to the server.

Cloud gaming was first envisioned in 2000 as a Wi-Fi service for handheld devices, but it took almost a decade for the infrastructure to catch up to the vision. In 2010 the first cloud gaming platform, OnLive, was launched in the United States, allowing game producers to run their creations on the OnLive servers. The launch

Steve Perlman, the founder of OnLive, stands in front of a display of his cloud gaming service. OnLive was launched in 2010, allowing game developers to run their creations on the company's servers. It was the first cloud gaming platform.

of OnLive opened the floodgates to other services, most notably Gaikai in 2011. Unlike OnLive, Gaikai allowed games to be embedded directly inside websites, on Facebook, or on mobile devices without requiring downloads, special plug-ins, or registration. A simple click on an enabled link or a visit to a Gaikai-powered game destination is all that is needed to activate the games. Sony acquired Gaikai and in 2013 revealed that it would use Gaikai to power cloud gaming services for the PlayStation 4, with the eventual aim of making the entire PlayStation catalogue available as a streaming service.

Social Networking

With the introduction of inexpensive Internet access and fast broadband connections, being "online"—connected to the Internet—has become infinitely easier, more affordable, and more "natural." Beyond being tools for finding information or accessing e-mail, as they had been with the dial-up modems of the 1990s, websites moved toward better user interfaces. Online developers sought to create online communities, the ultimate expression of which has been the rise of social networks.

As social networks have taken the world by storm, so, too, have social network games. Most social network games began as Internet browser games, but many are also available as apps for smartphones and tablets. With the proliferation of these devices, social network games such as *(lil) Green Patch*, *Happy Farm*, *Farm Town*, and *Mob Wars* have become some of the most popular games in the world, boasting tens of millions of players.

The earliest social network games were designed to be casual games featuring multiplayer play. Unlike many other types of video games where game play is resolved in real time, however, social network games do not require players to be online at the same time; instead, players take turns or finish the game and wait for their competitor to finish before seeing whether they have won. Players can use their social networks (either existing or emerging through the game play) to invite or challenge another player to a game.

Twitch Scratches an Itch

Launched in June 2011 as a live streaming video platform focused on video gaming, Twitch.tv boasts over 43 million viewers every month. Average viewers watch ninety minutes a day. Indeed, the website has become the most popular video game streaming service by a large margin. Max Gonzalez, a Twitch contributor, notes: "It's like a kind of talk show. Some people are watching just to hear me riff on the game. Some people are trying to pick up tips."

In February 2014 a video stream known as "Twitch Plays Pokémon"—a crowd-sourced attempt to play Pokémon Red using a system translating chat commands into game controls—went viral, reaching over 6.5 million views within five days and up to seventy thousand concurrent viewers, at least 10 percent of whom participated in the game. What made Twitch unique was its merging of video games with a participatory live video feed across multiple channels. "People have been watching people play video games since they were invented," says Emmett Shear, Twitch's chief executive. "If you think about old arcades, you spent much more time watching people play Pac Man than playing it yourself, because there weren't enough games to go around." As Twitch demonstrates, even with plenty of entertainment to go around, there will always be people who just want to watch.

Quoted in Chris O'Brien, "For Twitch, It's Game On," *Los Angeles Times*, May 25, 2014. www.latimes .com.

To entice users to play games more often, designers created goal-oriented social games that could continue indefinitely. *Clash of Clans*, for instance, which was designed specifically for cell phones and tablets, has many of the same role-playing features as the most successful MMORPGs such as players battling thousands of others in a virtual realm. Some social network games use the social network to facilitate game goals. In the eminently popular farming simulation game *FarmVille*, for example, players can entice online friends to join in the fun, either by playing themselves or passively by giving gifts or other game tokens to help out the player. Notably, *FarmVille*, which is available as an application via Facebook, is free to play, but the use of Farm Cash (or Farm Bucks in *FarmVille 2*)—purchased with a credit card or other "real-world" currency—greatly facilitates one's success.

Alternate Realities

The final frontier for online gaming—indeed for video games as a whole—may be virtual reality (VR), a computer-simulated environment that recreates a player's presence in places in the real world or imagined worlds. Although virtual reality has been imagined in movies, technical limitations on processing power, image resolution, and communication bandwidth have proved to be formidable obstacles to widespread application.

Current virtual reality environments tend to focus almost exclusively on the visual experience, but they may also include sound through speakers or headphones. Many early VR adopters have used the technology for military purposes, training a pilot or parachute jumper for combat, for instance. The first fully immersive virtual training system for soldiers was fielded at Fort Bragg in 2012. The program enables trainers to simulate missions or live-fire exercises in almost any environment that a soldier might encounter.

"People playing video games are like filmmakers—you can control the dream in your own living room. You create your own destiny; you become your own author."[45]

—*Adam Rapp, film director and Pulitzer Prize–runner-up playwright.*

The technology has moved beyond military use, however. The Oculus Rift, a new VR headset system designed for gaming, is in development, and early feedback has been positive. "The headset . . . makes the wearer feel as though he or she is literally living in a video game," writes Lauren Goode, who tried out the Oculus Rift at a trade show. "I could turn from side to side, or 360 degrees, and I was still immersed in the world inside the video game. . . . By 'walking' forward, or propelling myself with the controller, I could approach gun-toting characters within the video game, stare at them and walk through them. I could look up at the sky and down at the cobblestoned ground and see snow falling around me."[46]

As developers work out the kinks of the Oculus Rift (including price and gaming compatibility), other companies are exploring other possibilities to enhance the virtual reality experience. One thought on the horizon, for instance, is a one-directional treadmill that could enable players to simulate walking through a virtual world. With these and other VR products and technologies, in the not too distant future gamers may be able to immerse themselves even more fully in the realm of the video game developer's imagination.

Introduction: The Rise of Video Games

1. Mark J.P. Wolf, ed., *The Medium of the Video Game*. Austin: University of Texas Press, 2001, p. 14.

2. Nick Yee, "How The Media Consistently Gets Games Wrong," *The Blog, Huffington Post*, January 9, 2014. www.huffingtonpost.com.

3. Greg Perrault, "Why Do We Love Video Games?," *The Blog, Huffington Post*, February 10, 2014. www.huffingtonpost.com.

Chapter One: From the Laboratory to Main Street

4. Quoted in Harold Goldberg, *All Your Base Are Belong to Us: How Fifty Years of Videogames Conquered Pop Culture*. New York: Three Rivers, 2011, p. xix.

5. Stewart Brand, "Spacewar: Fanatic Life and Symbolic Death Among the Computer Bums," *Rolling Stone*, December 7, 1972, p. 52.

6. Quoted in Steven L. Kent, *The Ultimate History of Video Games: From Pong to Pokémon and Beyond—The Story Behind the Craze That Touched Our Lives and Changed the World*. New York: Random House, 2010, p. 23.

7. Quoted in *Video Game Invasion: The History of a Global Obsession*, TV documentary, directed by David Carr and David Comtois, 2004.

8. Henry Jenkins, "Getting into the Game," *EL Educational Leadership*, April 2005. www.ascd.org.

9. Linda Barton, personal interview by author, April 27, 2014.

10. Erkki Huhtamo, "What's Victoria Got to Do with It? Toward an Archaeology of Domestic Video Gaming," in Mark J.P. Wolf, *Before the Crash: Early Video Game History*. Detroit, MI: Wayne State University Press, 2012, p. 48.

11. Quoted in Travis Fahs, "The History of Activision," *IGN Magazine*, October 1, 2010. www.ign.com.

12. Quoted in *Snopes.com*, "Five Million E.T. Pieces," April 26, 2014. www.snopes.com.

13. Jon Freeman, "Should You Turn Pro?," *Computer Gaming World*, December 1984, p. 16.

14. bkturf, "Today in Gaming History: The NES Was Released to America in 1985," *Gaming*, 2014. www.reddit.com.

15. Carl Shapiro and Hal R. Varian, *Information Rules: A Strategic Guide to the Network Economy*. Cambridge, MA: Harvard Business Press, 1998, p. 178.

16. Sam Pettus et al., *Service Games: The Rise and Fall of SEGA: Enhanced Edition*," CreateSpace, 2013, p. 54.

17. YouTube, "Genesis Does What Nintendon't." www.youtube.com.

18. Kutter Callaway, "Wii Are Inspired: The Transformation of Home Video Gaming Consoles (and Us)," in Craig Detweiler, ed., *Halos and Avatars: Playing Video Games with God*. Westminster, UK: John Knox, 2010, p. 79.

19. Sony Computer Entertainment, "PlayStation 2 Breaks Record as the Fastest Computer Entertainment Platform to Reach Cumulative Shipment of 100 Million Units," press release, November 30, 2005. www.scei.co.jp.

20. IEEE Global History Network, "Gunpae Yokoi: Biography." www.ieeeghn.org.

21. Steven Williamson, "Nintendo Speech: We'd Hoped for More on the Revolution!," *Hexus*, March 24, 2006. hexus.net.

22. Quoted in *Businessweek*, in TCM News, "The Big Ideas Behind Nintendo's Wii," November 16, 2006. www.tmcnet.com.

23. Quoted in *Businessweek*, "The Big Ideas Behind Nintendo's Wii."

24. Perrault, "Why Do We Love Video Games?"

Chapter Three: In the Palm of Your Hand

25. Steven L. Kent, *The Ultimate History of Video Games*.

26. Quoted in Harold Goldberg, *All Your Base Are Belong to Us*.

27. Travis Fahs, "IGN Presents the History of Game Boy," IGN, July 27, 2009, p. 2. www.ign.com.

28. Daniel Sloan, *Playing to Wiin: Nintendo and the Video Game Industry's Greatest Comeback*. New York: Wiley, 2011, p. 66.

29. Jeff Ryan, *Super Mario: How Nintendo Conquered America*. New York: Penguin, 2011, p. 208.

30. Ryan, *Super Mario*, p. 209.

31. Quoted in Gloria Barczak and David Wesley, *Innovation and Marketing in the Video Game Industry: Avoiding the Performance Trap*. Surrey, UK: Gower, 2012, p. 45.

32. *Bloomberg Businessweek*, "Online Extra: Meet Mario's Papa," November 6, 2005. www.businessweek.com.

33. Joel Durham Jr., *Secrets of the PlayStation Portable*. Berkeley, CA: Peachpit, 2006, p. 7.

34. Larissa Hjorth, *Games and Gaming: An Introduction to New Media*. London: Berg, 2011, p. 41.

35. Quoted in Dan Steinbock, *The Mobile Revolution: The Making of Mobile Services Worldwide*. Miami, FL: Qualex Consulting Services, 2009, p. 154.

36. Andrew Kirmse, "History of *Meridian 59*, 1994–2004," *Meridian59*. http://meridian59.com.

37. Craig Detweiler, *Halos and Avatars: Playing Video Games with God*. Westminster, UK: John Knox, 2010, p. 113.

38. Quoted in Justin Olivetti, "The Game Archeologist Discovers the *Island of Kesmai*," Massively by Joystiq, March 6, 2012. http://massively.joystiq.com.

39. Olivetti, "The Game Archeologist Discovers the *Island of Kesmai*."

40. Kirmse, "History of Meridian 59, 1994–2004."

41. Quoted in Amanda Benson, "Jane McGonigal on How Computer Games Make You Smarter," *Smithsonian Magazine*, February 2011. www.smithsonianmag.com.

42. Allen Rausch and Miguel Lopez, "A History of D&D Video Games: Part II," GameSpy, August 16, 2004. www.gamespy.com.

43. Quoted in Media Education Foundation, *Game Over: Gender, Race & Violence in Video Games*, transcript, p. 4. www.mediaed.org.

44. Greg Kasavin, "Reviews: World of Warcraft," GameSpot, November 29, 2004. www.gamespot.com.

45. Quoted in Marsha Norman, "Adam Rapp," *Bomb*, Spring 2006. http://bombmagazine.org.

46. Lauren Goode, "Oculus Rift Virtual-Reality Headset Puts You Right in the Game," All Things D, January 11, 2013. http://allthingsd.com.

Related Organizations and Websites

Entertainment Consumers Association (ECA)

64 Danbury Rd., Suite 700
Wilton, CT 06897
phone: (203) 761-6180
fax: (203) 761-6184
e-mail: feedback@theeca.com
website: www.theeca.com

The ECA is a nonprofit organization that represents video game players. It is opposed to the regulation of video games based on content and supports the current system of self-regulation by the game industry. Its website contains facts and position papers about video games.

The Entertainment Software Association (ESA)

575 Seventh St. NW, Suite 300
Washington, DC 20004
e-mail: esa@theesa.com
website: www.theesa.com

The ESA is the trade association for the US computer and video game industry. Its website contains numerous research reports and facts and articles about video games.

International Center for the History of Electronic Games (ICHEG)

1 Manhattan Sq.
Rochester, NY 14607
phone: (585) 263-2700
website: www.icheg.org

The ICHEG collects, studies, and interprets video games and the ways in which these are changing how people, play, learn, and connect with one another.

Media Education Foundation

60 Masonic St.
Northampton, MA 01060
phone: (800) 897-0089
fax: (800) 659-6882
e-mail: info@mediaed.org
website: http://mediaed.org

The Media Education Foundation provides educational videos about media, culture, and society for the classroom.

Media Smarts

950 Gladstone Ave., Suite 120
Ottawa, ON
Canada K1Y 3E6
phone: (613) 224-7721 or (800)-896-3342
fax: (613) 761-9024
e-mail: info@mediasmarts.ca
website: http://mediasmarts.ca

MediaSmarts is a Canadian not-for-profit charitable organization for digital and media literacy.

Books

Tom Bissell, *Extra Lives: Why Video Games Matter*. New York: Pantheon, 2010.

Harold Goldberg, *All Your Base Are Belong to Us: How Fifty Years of Videogames Conquered Pop Culture*. New York: Three Rivers, 2011.

Blake Harris, *Console Wars: Sega, Nintendo, and the Battle That Defined a Generation*. New York: HarperCollins, 2014.

Steven L. Kent, *The Ultimate History of Video Games: From Pong to Pokémon and Beyond—The Story Behind the Craze That Touched Our Lives and Changed the World*. New York: Three Rivers, 2010.

Steven Levy, *Hackers: Heroes of the Computer Revolution* 25th anniversary ed. Sebastopol, CA: O'Reilly, 2010.

Sam Pettus et al., *Service Games: The Rise and Fall of SEGA* Enhanced ed. Google eBook, 2013.

Jeff Ryan, *Super Mario: How Nintendo Conquered America*. New York: Penguin, 2011.

Mark J.P. Wolf, ed., *Before the Crash: Early Video Game History*. Detriot: Wayne State University Press, 2012.

Mark J.P. Wolf, ed., *Encyclopedia of Video Games: The Culture, Technology, and Art of Gaming*. Santa Barbara, CA: Greenwood, 2012.

Nick Yee, *The Proteus Paradox: How Online Games and Virtual Worlds Change Us and How They Don't*. New Haven, CT: Yale University Press, 2014.

Internet Sources

Atari Historical Society. www.atarimuseum.com/mainmenu/main menu.html.

Computer History Museum. www.computerhistory.org/timeline /?category=cmptr.

The DANA Foundation, "Video Games Affect the Brain—for Better and Worse." www.dana.org/Cerebrum/2009/Video_Games_Affect _the_Brain%E2%80%94for_Better_and_Worse.

Games Radar, "The 100 Best Games of All Time." www.gamesradar .com/best-games-ever.

GameSided, "Top 20 Mobile Games of All Time." http://gamesided .com/2013/08/24/top-20-mobile-games-of-all-time.

GameSpot. www.gamespot.com.

History of Computing. http://mason.gmu.edu/~montecin/computer -hist-web.htm.

International Center for the History of Electronic Games, "Video Game History Timeline." www.icheg.org/icheg-game-history/time line.

PBS, "The Video Game Revolution." www.pbs.org/kcts/videogame revolution/history.

ProCon.org, "Video Games." http://videogames.procon.org.

Video Game Console Library. www.videogameconsolelibrary.com.

Video Games: History, Open Directory Project. www.dmoz.org /Games/Video_Games/History.

About the Author

Lydia Bjornlund is a freelance writer and editor living in northern Virginia. She has written more than two dozen nonfiction books for children and teens, mostly on American history and health-related topics. She also writes books and training materials for adults on issues related to conservation and public management, as well as educational testing and curriculum materials. Bjornlund holds a master's degree in education from Harvard University and a bachelor of arts degree in American Studies from Williams College. She lives with her husband, Gerry Hoetmer, and their children, Jake and Sophia. The author extends a sincere thank you to Harold Alby for his help in researching and writing this book.